LANGUAGE ARTS EXPLORER JUNIOR

How to Write an E-mail

by Cecilia Minden
and Kate Roth

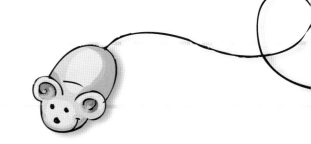

CHERRY LAKE PUBLISHING · ANN ARBOR, MICHIGAN

CHERRY LAKE

Publishing

Published in the United States of America by Cherry Lake Publishing
Ann Arbor, Michigan
www.cherrylakepublishing.com

Content Adviser: Jeannette Mancilla-Martinez, EdD, Assistant Professor of
Literacy, Language, and Culture, University of Illinois at Chicago

Design and Illustration: The Design Lab

Photo Credits: Page 4, ©iStockphoto.com/morganl; page 10, ©Justin
Paget/Shutterstock, Inc.; page 13, ©Ivonne Wierink/Shutterstock, Inc.;
page 17, ©iStockphoto.com/browndogstudios; page 21, ©iofoto/
Shutterstock, Inc.

Library of Congress Cataloging-in-Publication Data
Minden, Cecilia.
  How to write an email/by Cecilia Minden and Kate Roth.
    p. cm.
  Includes bibliographical references and index.
  ISBN-13: 978-1-60279-993-6 (lib. bdg.)
  ISBN-13: 978-1-61080-275-8 (pbk.)
  1. Electronic mail messages—Juvenile literature. 2. Online
etiquette—Juvenile literature. I. Roth, Kate. II. Title.
  TK5105.73.M56 2011
  004.692—dc22   2010030065

Cherry Lake Publishing would like to acknowledge the work
of The Partnership for 21st Century Skills. Please visit
www.21stcenturyskills.org for more information.

Printed in the United States of America
Corporate Graphics Inc.
July 2011
CLFA09

Table of Contents

CHAPTER ONE
You've Got Mail!. 4

CHAPTER TWO
From Me to You. 6

CHAPTER THREE
Keep It Friendly 10

CHAPTER FOUR
Extras 14

CHAPTER FIVE
And Another Thing 18

CHAPTER SIX
That Was Easy!. 21

Glossary. 22
For More Information 23
Index 24
About the Authors. 24

You've Got Mail!

E-mail can be a great way to keep in touch with friends and family members.

Electronic mail, or e-mail, is an important part of our world. E-mails are messages. They are sent and read using computers and other tools.

Once you send an e-mail, you can't take it back. That is why you must get your e-mails just right. Let's find out how!

Be Safe

Be safe when using e-mail and the Internet.
Remember these points:

1. Follow school and home rules of computer safety.
2. Ask an adult you trust before sharing personal facts about yourself in an e-mail. These include your name and address.
3. Never talk to strangers online or agree to meet in person.
4. Tell an adult if you see anything online that makes you feel uncomfortable.

Smart Web surfers follow Internet safety rules.

CHAPTER TWO

From Me to You

Do you have an e-mail address? If not, an adult can help you set up an **e-mail account**. Your parents may set up special controls. These controls are meant to keep you safe. For example, you may only be able to send e-mails to family members and friends.

Ask an adult to help you set up an e-mail account.

Think of a creative username.

One part of an e-mail address is the username. You may be able to make yours up. Think of something fun for your username. Don't use your full name. Imagine a girl named Kasey. She plays the piano. She might use kplayskeys as her username. Her email address would be *kplayskeys@xyz.com*.

Think of a friend you would like to e-mail. Let's send that person a message. Here's what you'll need to complete the activities in this book:

- A computer that is connected to the Internet
- An e-mail account

Addressing an E-mail

INSTRUCTIONS:
1. Open your e-mail account.
2. Click on the "New" button. A message window should appear.
3. Look for the "To:" box. This is where you enter the addresses of the person who will receive your message. Type your friend's e-mail address in this space.
4. The "Cc:" box is next. *Cc* stands for "**carbon copy**." A copy of the e-mail is sent to addresses entered here. Do you want someone else to read this e-mail? Enter his or her address in the "Cc:" box.
5. Look for the "Subject:" box. This lets the receiver know the topic of your e-mail. Type in the "Subject:" space. Your subject line should only be a few words long.

On to the next step of writing an e-mail!

SEND ATTACH ADDRESSES FONTS COLOR SIZE

From: soccergirl@xyz.com
To: kplayskeys@xyz.com
Cc:
Bcc:
Subject: Party at the Library

Are you entering more than one address in a "To:" or "Cc:" box? Put a comma between each e-mail address.

You may also come across a "Bcc:" box. *Bcc* stands for "Blind carbon copy." Using this tool lets you send a copy of the e-mail to someone in secret. Others who receive the message can't see the addresses entered in this space.

CHAPTER THREE

Keep It Friendly

Choose your words carefully in an e-mail. You do not want to hurt someone's feelings.

Think about talking to a friend face-to-face. You can see if she understands you. In an e-mail, the person only sees your words. Never write an e-mail when you are angry. Take some time to cool down. How is writing an e-mail different? The person only sees your words.

Sometimes the words you choose can have two meanings. Be sure your true meaning is clear. For example, a friend e-mails you a picture of his new haircut. You respond by saying, "That's wild!" You mean that you think it is a great haircut. Could your friend think it means something else?

Are you asking questions in your e-mail? Read them out loud. Are the questions clear? Will the reader understand?

Be careful what you type!

ACTIVITY

Writing an E-mail

INSTRUCTIONS:

1. Begin your e-mail with a greeting. *Hi* and *Dear* are common greetings, followed by the reader's name. Put a comma after the name.
2. Next, type the body of your e-mail. This is where you share your news. E-mails are usually short. Try to word your message in a few sentences.
3. Type a closing after the body. It is a way of saying good-bye. *Thanks,* and *Sincerely,* are two closings. Put a comma after the closing. Type your name on the line after the closing.

Hi!

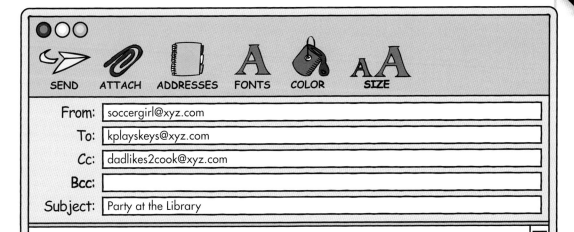

From: soccergirl@xyz.com

To: kplayskeys@xyz.com

Cc: dadlikes2cook@xyz.com

Bcc:

Subject: Party at the Library

Hi Kasey,

The author party at the library is this Saturday. Our favorite author will be there. Dad said we could pick you up on Saturday morning. The party starts at noon. Maybe we can get our books signed!

Can you go?

Talk to you soon,
Taylor

P.S. Check out this picture of a sand castle I made at the beach.

CHAPTER FOUR

Extras

You can change the look of your e-mails. How? You can use different **fonts**, colors, and **emoticons**. Fonts are sets of letters and numbers of a certain size and style. An emoticon is a group of marks that shows how you feel.

Can you guess what these emoticons mean?

Jazz Up Your E-mail

INSTRUCTIONS:

How you change fonts and colors depends on your e-mail **program**. Here is one way:

1. Go back to the e-mail you wrote earlier. Use the computer mouse to highlight your message. Click on the "Font" list. You will see a list of fonts. Choose one.

2. Click on the "Font Size" list. Do you see a list of numbers? These are font sizes. Choose a size.

3. You can also change the color of your font. Click on the "Font Color" button. Choose a color.

4. Add an emoticon after a sentence. Want to show that you are happy? Type a colon, a **hyphen**, and a right **parenthesis**. Your emoticon should look like this: :-) Do you see a smiley face?

From: soccergirl@xyz.com

To: kplayskeys@xyz.com

Cc: dadlikes2cook@xyz.com

Bcc:

Subject: Party at the Library

Hi Kasey,

The author party at the library is this Saturday. Our FAVORITE author will be there. Dad said we could pick you up on Saturday morning. The party starts at noon. Maybe we can get our books signed! :-)

CAN YOU GO?

Talk to you soon,
Taylor

P.S. Check out this picture of a sand castle I made at the beach.

Some e-mail programs include a row of pictures called **icons**. If your program has icons, you can click on the icons to change the font size, font color, and add emoticons.

CHAPTER FIVE

And Another Thing

Attachments are files that you send with an e-mail. Pictures are one kind of attachment.

Attachments

Let's attach a picture to the e-mail. Check with an adult before sharing any pictures with other people.

INSTRUCTIONS:

1. How you attach a file depends on your e-mail program. In some programs, you click on a button that says "Attach Files." Sometimes, this button only has a paper clip icon. Click the correct button for your program.
2. Find the file you need in the window that appears. Click on it. Click the button in this window that attaches the file to your e-mail. It may be called "Choose" or something similar.

From: soccergirl@xyz.com

To: kplayskeys@xyz.com

Cc: dadlikes2cook@xyz.com

Bcc:

Subject: Party at the Library

Talk to you Soon,
Taylor

P.S. Check out this picture of a sand castle I made at the beach.

You are almost ready to send your e-mail. First, you must look it over.

Final Changes

1. Read your e-mail carefully. Read it out loud. Check everything one more time:

☐ YES ☐ NO Are the e-mail addresses correct?
☐ YES ☐ NO Did I fill in the "Subject:" box?
☐ YES ☐ NO Is there a greeting and a closing?
☐ YES ☐ NO Is the body clear and easy to follow?
☐ YES ☐ NO Does my true meaning come across?
☐ YES ☐ NO Did I play with fonts or use emoticons?
☐ YES ☐ NO Are the words spelled correctly?
☐ YES ☐ NO Did I attach the correct file?

2. Make changes to your e-mail if needed.

All that is left is to send your e-mail on its way. Hit the "Send" button!

CHAPTER SIX

That Was Easy!

Your friend will be glad to get an e-mail from you. Soon, you may get a reply.

Writing e-mails is fun and easy. Are you already thinking about your next e-mail?

You can send an e-mail to anyone who has an e-mail address.

Glossary

attachments (uh-TACH-muhntss) files that are sent with e-mails

carbon copy (KAR-buhn KOP-ee) a copy of an e-mail sent to people other than the main receivers of the message

electronic mail (i-lek-TRON-ik MAYL) messages sent over the Internet or special computer systems

e-mail account (EE-mayl uh-KOUNT) a setup that allows users to send and receive e-mail

emoticons (i-MOH-ti-konz) groups of marks used to show how you feel

fonts (FAHNTS) sets of letters and numbers of a certain size and style

hyphen (HYE-fuhn) a punctuation mark (-) used in words made of two or more parts

icons (EYE-konz) tiny pictures on computer screens that stand for programs, actions, and other things

parenthesis (puh-REN-thuh-siss) one of a pair of special curved lines ( ) used in writing

program (PROH-gram) the instructions that control how a computer works

username (YOO-zur-naym) the part of an e-mail address to the left of the "at" (@) sign

For More Information

BOOKS

Jakubiak, David J. *A Smart Kid's Guide to Internet Privacy*. New York: PowerKids Press, 2010.

Oxlade, Chris. *My First E-mail Guide*. Chicago: Heinemann Library, 2007.

WEB SITES

FBI—Internet Safety
www.fbi.gov/kids/k5th/safety2.htm
Find tips for staying safe online.

PBS Kids—E-mail
pbskids.org/arthur/games/letterwriter/email.html
Look here to learn more about the parts of an e-mail.

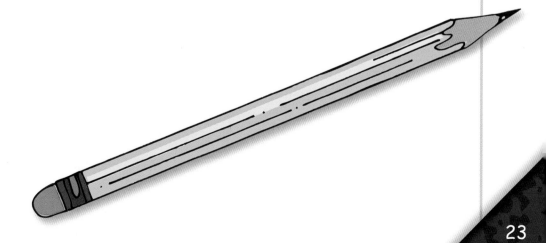

Index

accounts, 6, 7, 8
addresses, 5, 6, 7, 8, 9,
    20
anger, 10
attachments, 18, 20

"Bcc:" box, 9
body, 12, 20

"Cc:" box, 8, 9
closings, 12, 20
colors, 14, 15, 17

emoticons, 14, 15, 17, 20

fonts, 14, 15, 17, 20

greetings, 12, 20

icons, 17, 18

meaning, 11, 20

name, 5, 7, 12
"New" button, 8

parents, 6
personal facts, 5
pictures, 17, 18

programs, 15, 17, 18

safety, 5, 6
"Send" button, 20
special controls, 6
spelling, 20
strangers, 5
"Subject:" box, 8, 20

"To:" box, 8, 9

usernames, 7

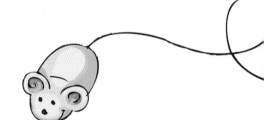

About the Authors

Cecilia Minden, PhD, is the former Director of the Language and Literacy Program at Harvard Graduate School of Education. While at Harvard, Dr. Minden taught several writing courses for teachers. She is now a full-time literacy consultant and the author of more than 100 books for children. Dr. Minden lives in Chapel Hill, North Carolina, with her husband, Dave Cupp, and a cute but spoiled Yorkie named Kenzie.

Kate Roth has a doctorate from Harvard University in Language and Literacy and a masters from Columbia University Teachers College in Curriculum and Teaching. Her work focuses on writing instruction in the primary grades. She has taught first grade, kindergarten, and Reading Recovery. She has also instructed hundreds of teachers from around the world in early literacy practices. She lives in Shanghai, China, with her husband and three children, ages 2, 6, and 9. They do a lot of writing to stay in touch with friends and family and record their experiences.